TECH **TITANS**

GOOGLE

BY AUDREY DeANGELIS AND GINA DeANGELIS

CONTENT CONSULTANT

Anthony Rotolo
Media Scholar, Speaker, and Consultant

Essential Library

An Imprint of Abdo Publishing | abdobooks.com

ABDOBOOKS.COM

Published by Abdo Publishing, a division of ABDO, PO Box 398166, Minneapolis, Minnesota 55439. Copyright © 2019 by Abdo Consulting Group, Inc. International copyrights reserved in all countries. No part of this book may be reproduced in any form without written permission from the publisher. Essential Library™ is a trademark and logo of Abdo Publishing.

Printed in the United States of America, North Mankato, Minnesota.
072018
012019

Cover Photo: Glenn Chapman/AFP/Getty Images
Interior Photos: Shutterstock Images, 4–5; Red Line Editorial, 7; Elise Amendola/AP Images, 9; Paul Sakuma/AP Images, 13; Jonathan Elderfield/Hulton Archive/Getty Images, 14–15; Dario Lopez-Mills/AP Images, 16; Shutterstock Images, 20; Jeramey Lende/Shutterstock Images, 25; Kim Kulish/Corbis Historical/Getty Images, 26–27; John Cogill/AP Images, 30; PeopleImages/iStockphoto, 35; Craig Mitchelldyer/Getty Images, 37; iStockphoto, 38–39; Paul Sakuma/AP Images, 41; Red Line Editorial, 45; Mark Lennihan/AP Images, 49; iStockphoto, 52–53; UGUR CAN/AFP/Getty Images, 55; Ng Han Guan/AP Images, 58; Elizabeth Dalziel/AP Images, 61; Keith Bedford/Bloomberg/Getty Images, 62–63; Tom Williams/CQ Roll Call/AP Images, 68; Mary Altaffer/AP Images, 72; Ben Margot/AP Images, 74–75; Justin Sullivan/Getty Images News/Getty Images, 78; Joshua Boucher/News Herald/AP Images, 80; Marcio Jose Sanchez/AP Images, 85; Ore Huiying/Bloomberg/Getty Images, 86–87; Tobias Schwarz/AFP/Getty Images, 90; John Minchillo/AP Images, 94; Red Line Editorial, 97

Editor: Arnold Ringstad
Series Designer: Laura Polzin

Library of Congress Control Number: 2018948246

Publisher's Cataloging-in-Publication Data

Names: DeAngelis, Audrey, author. | DeAngelis, Gina, author.
Title: Google / by Audrey DeAngelis and Gina DeAngelis.
Description: Minneapolis, Minnesota : Abdo Publishing, 2019 | Series: Tech titans | Includes online resources and index.
Identifiers: ISBN 9781532116889 (lib. bdg.) | ISBN 9781532159725 (ebook)
Subjects: LCSH: Google (Firm)--Juvenile literature. | Web search engines--Juvenile literature. | Computers--Juvenile literature. | Technology--Juvenile literature.
Classification: DDC 338.470040--dc23

CONTENTS

CHAPTER ONE

ORGANIZING THE WORLD'S INFORMATION

Today, Google is the number one search engine in the United States and in the world. The company has more than 72,000 employees. It made more than $19 billion in profit in 2017. It owns YouTube, the number one online video site. It owns the Android smartphone operating system, which is used by more than two billion people every month.[1] Google has worked with other companies to design smartphones and Chromebooks, slimmed-down laptops that use Google's own web browser, Chrome.

From its earliest days, Google has been known for innovation. Even now, as one of the world's largest companies, it still pushes the boundaries of technology. Google employees

Google has gone from a company started by a pair of college students to a multibillion-dollar company that controls access to a vast amount of information.

work to make self-driving cars widely available. Google engineers work with the National Aeronautics and Space Administration (NASA) to help discover new planets. One of the company's projects is to build a system of huge balloons to give internet access to the whole world.

People around the world run an average of more than 40,000 internet searches on Google.com every second. That's more than three billion searches every day.[2] Each one of those people is looking for some specific information, and Google's technology scours the internet to find the answers users are seeking. Of all the online search traffic in the world in 2017, more than 80 percent of it was through Google.[3] Users can search for—and within—scholarly articles and books, news items, videos, or across the entire World Wide Web at once.

Google, now officially a part of the parent company Alphabet Inc., is one of the world's largest and most influential technology companies. It provides billions of people with software, services, and free access to the world's collected knowledge. It may be surprising, then, to learn that Google began as a student project in the mid-1990s at Stanford University. How did Google become the tech titan it is today?

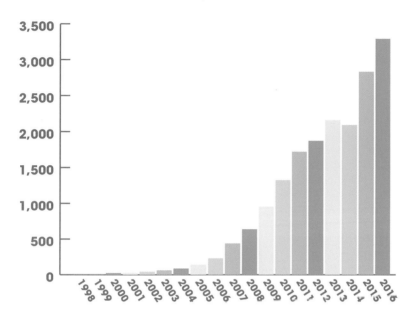

GOOGLE SEARCHES, 1998–2016 (BILLIONS)[4]

THE INTERNET AND THE WEB

The idea of the internet developed in the mid-1900s. At the time, computers were huge, expensive, and complex. Only laboratories, certain government agencies, and a few universities had them. Researchers in these places wanted to find a way for their computers to communicate with each other. They created a closed network using telephone lines and created software protocols to transfer data between computers.

Then, during the 1970s and 1980s, computers became smaller, less expensive, and easier to use. More and more people began to use them. In just a few years, the internet spread to more universities and businesses, and eventually to the general public. Even so, the internet required technical expertise to access, and it didn't look anything like it does today.

English computer scientist Tim Berners-Lee realized the internet needed to be easier for more people to use. In 1989, he proposed the World Wide Web, a network of linked pages and files that could be accessed using the internet. He created a new standardized protocol to let computers talk to each other—the hypertext transfer protocol (HTTP). He also created hypertext markup language (HTML), a standardized format in which pages on the World

MORE THAN A SEARCH ENGINE

Today, almost every part of a person's digital life can be lived through Google services or on Google devices. Chat programs such as Allo and Hangouts use text and video. Google Maps provides navigation directions and traffic information. Google Books is a digital library bigger than any physical library in existence. Documents are created, saved, and shared through Google Docs and Google Drive. Millions of users browse the web with Google Chrome. Papers are submitted and graded through Google Classroom. Classes can take virtual reality field trips through Expeditions. And in its Google Play Store, the company sells games, music, television shows, and movies.

Berners-Lee invented the World Wide Web while working at the European Organization for Nuclear Research (CERN, in its French acronym).

Wide Web could be written. Using HTML would mean that pages would display in the same way for all users, regardless of what kind of computer they were using. The first website went live in 1991. Central to the World Wide Web were hyperlinks, pieces of text on a website that could be clicked to take the user to a different, related page. Hyperlinks soon connected vast numbers of documents on the web. In 1993, Berners-Lee's research organization put the software for the web into the public domain, making it free for anyone to use. By 1995, there were already about ten million documents on the World Wide Web.[5] Berners-Lee's work set the stage for the modern information age.

NAVIGATING THE WEB

Around this time, Larry Page and Sergey Brin were students at Stanford University in California. They were working toward PhDs in computer science. They came up with a new idea to help people find what they were looking for online. Their system would analyze how popular websites were, then use that information to help rank them in search results.

In the process, the young men developed a new way of searching the web. They called their search engine Google, a deliberate misspelling of the word *googol*, which is a number equal to one followed by 100 zeros. The first version went live on the Stanford University website in 1997. It had a refreshingly clean look, it was simple to use, and it had no ads. In 1998, Page and Brin decided to leave school to start their own company.

GOOGLE GROWS

The site's popularity grew fast. *Google* became a common term meaning "to conduct a computer search."[6] In 2006, it was even added to the *Oxford English Dictionary*. For a long time, people wondered how a search engine company could make money. After all, a good search engine sent users away from the search engine to the website they were looking for. But Google stayed in business, at first relying on investments. When Google did eventually start to show advertisements, they were separated from search results, and they only appeared when they were related to the search terms. The enormous volume of searches that happen every day means this advertising revenue adds up to billions of dollars per year.

STANFORD START-UPS

In the 1980s and 1990s, Stanford University was a good place for people to start a tech company. The university had an Office of Technology Licensing. It helped students get patents to protect their inventions. Located in Silicon Valley, the heart of the tech industry, Stanford is surrounded by venture capitalists. These people invest large amounts of money to help new companies. Stanford also allowed its professors to keep a stake in any companies formed from projects they advised.

Many computer companies came from this environment. In the 1980s came Sun Microsystems, a company that developed computer hardware and software. Its cofounder Andy Bechtolsheim gave Google its first $100,000 check.[7] In the 1990s came Excite, a search company founded by Stanford alumni, and Yahoo!, an information directory and search company founded by two Stanford PhD candidates.

Over the last two decades, Google has changed the way the world thinks of computers and the internet. As a result of the company's success, Google can carry out major projects intended to advance the world's access to technology. For example, the company embarked on a project to digitize entire college libraries, making them accessible and searchable to everyone. This project changed the way people do research. People can access this information from anywhere with an internet connection.

In 2004, the company offered a mission statement for investors: "To do great things for the world."[8] Some people worry that Google's "great things" present dangers to personal privacy or that the company controls too much information. But however people feel about Google, it is clear that what started in a college dorm room a few decades ago has changed the world.

SERGEY BRIN AND LARRY PAGE

It made sense that Sergey Brin and Larry Page would end up working together. They grew up with similar backgrounds, and both are brilliant and determined.

Brin's father was a mathematician and professor, and his mother was a NASA scientist. When he was a child, Brin and his family immigrated to the United States from Russia. Brin graduated from college when he was 19, years younger than most students, and started graduate school at Stanford University in 1994. Despite his young age, he passed all his required exams within his first year so he could take the classes he wanted.

For his part, Page was interested in computers from an early age. His father taught computer science and his mother taught computer programming at Michigan State University. As a first grader, Page was the first student in his class to turn in a paper written and printed from a computer. And he once took apart all of the household power tools to see how they worked. His parents were angry because he couldn't put them back together.

By 2018, Brin, *left*, and Page, *right*, would become two of the wealthiest people on the planet.

CHAPTER TWO

A NEW WAY TO SEARCH

When Page and Brin started studying for their PhDs in computer science at Stanford University, most people were just starting to hear about the World Wide Web. At the time, most internet users simply accessed bulletin board services or sent emails to each other. But that was changing quickly. The first popular web browser, called Mosaic, launched in 1993. Now more people had a way to easily explore the web. More access meant more people could create more websites. In the first year after Mosaic was released, the number of pages on the web grew from about 130 to 2,700.[1]

At this point, companies started to create web portals. These websites featured pages for news, games, discussion forums, sports, and other information. The idea was to keep users on the website as long as possible. Companies

In the early days of the web, some users went to internet cafés to get online.

Jerry Yang cofounded Yahoo! in 1994 while a graduate student at Stanford University.

wanted their websites to be major destinations for web users. Some portals, such as Yahoo!, featured directories. These were lists of websites that users could visit, organized by topic. Rather than enter a search query to get a list of related pages, users clicked through lists of topics and subtopics until they found something they wanted. As the internet kept growing, though, the directory system wasn't enough. There were just too many pages. Looking through them for a certain piece of information could take hours.

In 1996, Yahoo! partnered with AltaVista, an internet search engine, to add a search function to Yahoo!'s website. Other popular search sites at that time included Lycos, Dogpile, and Ask Jeeves. These searches all worked mostly the same way: users typed in a word or words and then the web pages that used those words the most came up as search results. Matching words can be a useful tool sometimes, but in other cases it does not work well. Some people learned how to manipulate this kind of search. They would embed words on their websites that were not visible to users but would be detected by search engines. This could artificially boost a website's ranking in a search.

This search-ranking issue was the problem that Page set out to solve. One way to figure out the influence of an academic paper is to see how many other papers use it as a source. This is hard to track on paper, but with a network of computers, it was much easier. The same idea, Page believed, could be applied to websites. The more links to a page, the more people think that site is important. For example, if 15 websites link to website A, and only five link to website B, then website A might be a more reliable or useful source.

In the early 1990s, the popular search site AltaVista already tracked these links between web pages. But AltaVista didn't use that information in its search results. Page realized that using those links could help determine which sites were most trusted and useful. Page wanted to use those links, as well as matching words, to rank the search results. The best ones would go at the top of the list.

ALTAVISTA: THE FIRST RIVAL

Prior to Google's arrival on the scene, a variety of other online search engines were available to the public. Yahoo!, Excite, and Netscape were popular, but AltaVista had the most users. Louis Monier, one of its key designers, realized that speeding up the crawling process would improve the search service. Instead of processing one page at a time, his system processed a thousand at a time. By late 1995, when Monier convinced his bosses to make the search engine available to the public, most big search engines had indexed one million documents. AltaVista had indexed 16 million.[2] That made it the most useful search engine out there, at least until Google came along.

CRAWLING AND RANKING

In 1996, Page started writing a program that would collect all of these links. To collect them, he had to download the contents of the entire web. This part of the search is done by a crawler, a program that follows links around the web, downloading each page and tracking where all the links go.

Page soon had far more information than he could easily sort. It became a mathematical problem. He received help from his friend Brin. Brin was studying for a PhD at Stanford. He helped figure out how to use the information Page was collecting. The sheer amount of data meant more disk drives were needed to store all of it. Soon, Page's dorm room was full of computer drives. Brin's living room became Google's first office.

Meanwhile, Page kept working on an algorithm to rank various websites based on links. But, it turned out, there was another problem. According to Page, "The early versions of hypertext had a tragic flaw: you couldn't follow links in the other direction."[3] If website A linked to website B, users of website B wouldn't necessarily see anything linking back to website A. That was another problem Page wanted to solve. He created a new program, which he called BackRub, to study how pages linked back to each other.

BackRub was later renamed PageRank, after Page himself. It had yet another problem to solve. What if the five sites linking to website B were more reliable than the fifteen sites linking to website A? That made website B the more useful one. It is not just the number of references that matter but also where those references come from.

Google got its start on the campus of Stanford University in California.

So, Page's program worked backward to explore how many pages linked to all of those reference pages, and how many pages linked to those references' references. Developing the algorithms for the program to do this was difficult and ambitious. But Page and Brin were sure they could do it.

GOOGLE IS BORN

Page and Brin worked together with research assistants Scott Hassan and Alan Steremberg. The four developed a way to search the internet so that the most relevant results would show up first. They named their new search engine Google. Their search function went live on the Stanford University website in August 1997. Within a few months, Google was processing about 10,000 search queries per day.[4]

Hassan told Page and Brin that they should turn Google into a company, but they weren't ready to leave school. In 1996, even before the search engine went live on Stanford's website, they decided to offer their program to other companies, such as Yahoo!, Excite, and even AltaVista. But none of these companies were interested. Search engines made money by showing advertisements. The sooner users found what they were looking for, the sooner they left the search page, and the fewer ads they would see. In a way, executives from Excite and Yahoo! turned them down because Google was too good.

Page and Brin eventually decided to form their own company in 1998. They were encouraged by Brin's academic adviser, who reminded him that they could always come back to school to finish their PhDs if Google didn't work out. But at that point, if Google were to continue, it needed to move off campus. The crawler had been running for two years, and by then

WHEN GOOGLE FELL APART

When Larry Page was still in grade school, he built a computer printer out of Lego blocks. Years later, at Stanford, he built the skeleton of Google's first computer out of an off-brand block set similar to Duplo blocks. Because these blocks didn't lock together well, the structure would occasionally fall apart and take down the entire search system.

But the blocks weren't the only thing that brought down the system. Because they were in school, Page and Brin didn't have the money to buy new equipment. Instead they begged for what they could get from around campus. They bought cheap computers and parts. Things occasionally broke. But this pushed Page and Brin to design a system that would reroute a search query around a broken computer and return results anyway.

it had downloaded more than 24 million web pages.[5] Google was running from the Stanford website, and with 10,000 searches per day, it was slowing down the university's network.[6]

In 1998, Page and Brin moved their operation into a garage and two rooms they rented from a Stanford graduate, Susan Wojcicki. With a tight budget, it was important for Page and Brin to save money. They laid doors on top of sawhorses to create desks. They put a sign outside the garage that said, "Google Worldwide Headquarters."[7] The move meant they had new bills to pay, since the university didn't cover their costs anymore. Page and Brin would need financial help. Fortunately, being off campus also meant they were able to look for investors for the new company.

Early investors were
starting to bring in money, but
with a constantly increasing
amount of data, Google always
needed more equipment. In
2000, the company signed a
contract to provide search
services for the internal
servers of software company
Red Hat for $20,000 a month.[8]
Red Hat in turn provided
software and hardware for the
growing company.

EARLY PRIVACY CONCERNS

SUSAN WOJCICKI

In 1998, Susan Wojcicki had just earned her master's degree in business administration. Brin and Page offered to rent space in her garage and house to use as their new company's office. According to Wojcicki, the Google founders were good tenants. The next year, Google hired Wojcicki to handle marketing. "It wasn't clear what I was supposed to do," she said later, because Page and Brin refused to advertise the company.[9] Still, Wojcicki has been a key executive since Google's beginning. In 2014, Wojcicki became chief executive officer (CEO) of YouTube, which Google owns.

There were downsides to this early success, though. Since
its early days, Google has caused people to be concerned
about their privacy. When Page's crawler first started
downloading the web page by page, some website
owners worried that it was stealing their property. The
crawler went through each of their pages faster than
a real person could, and sometimes it overloaded the
website and caused it to crash. One art museum thought

that the crawler was going to steal photos of its art and post them elsewhere on the internet. Page tried to explain that the crawler wasn't stealing anything, and he built in a small bit of code that these website owners could use to prevent his crawler from scanning their pages. However, that wasn't enough to stop Stanford from getting lots of messages from angry website owners. Stanford's officer of risk management also contacted Page and Brin after receiving angry calls and letters about Google.

As Google's search engine and database grew, these concerns continued, and others arose. People who had spent many years carefully hiding personal information found it suddenly available to anyone through a Google search. This included addresses for victims of domestic abuse or details of criminal charges, whether proven or unproven. Page and Brin argued that they weren't the ones who put that information on the internet in the first place. In order for Google to bring it up with a search, it had to have already been on the web. And, as they continued to argue through the years, any human interference in what search results were returned would slow down the site and ruin the public's trust in Google's impartiality. Unless there were a legal reason to take something out of the search results, they said, it would

Google search result pages soon became a common sight for nearly every web user.

stay there. But these troubles, along with questions about how Google handles users' privacy, were just the beginning.

CHAPTER THREE

HIRING AND GROWING

Google started hiring employees in 1998, around the time it moved into Wojcicki's garage. Page and Brin wanted to make sure they hired not just people who were talented but also those who wouldn't be stopped by focusing on how things had been done before. That's why many of their employees started working for Google right out of college. Some of their first hires were from Stanford University.

Google still has very strict hiring practices, although the process has been streamlined since the company's early years. At first, the entire company was involved in hiring new employees. Even as the company grew to thousands of people, Page, Brin, or other top executives were still required to sign off for someone to be hired. They wanted to make sure that they were hiring

Even as the company grew, Page and Brin continued to closely monitor the hiring process.

good people, but this requirement slowed down the hiring process. The company also lacked older employees, valued for their knowledge and experience. In 2004, the average age of Google employees was under 30 years old. Only two out of every 100 employees were over the age of 40.[1]

COMPANY CULTURE

Page and Brin questioned normal office environments as much as they questioned the old way of running internet searches. They encouraged a relaxed atmosphere from the beginning. Even today, Google employees, which the company calls Googlers, tend to wear casual clothes rather than business suits. Page and Brin also rejected a strict hierarchy among most of their staff. Instead of reporting to a boss who reports to another boss and so on, Google programmers work in teams. All report to the same person. The teams change periodically.

This structure is about more than just who is in charge. The idea is that if everyone is on the same level, employees won't worry as much about sharing their ideas or disagreeing with their boss. Then information can flow more freely. A flat organization still presents challenges, though. The company must hire employees who are able to work independently without always being told what to do.

From the beginning, Page and Brin provided food for their employees. At first this meant granola bars and juice, but as Google grew, so did the office budget. In 1999, the company hired a chef to offer breakfast, lunch, and dinner to employees, paid for entirely by the company. Break rooms continued to be stocked with juices and snacks, even as Google expanded into multiple buildings. Eventually the Google campus contained 18 cafés and restaurants.[2] Google continues to offer meals to its employees, though during the 2008 recession it cut back on the number of restaurants and their hours.

Part of the reason for providing good food at the office wasn't just to be whimsical or attract more employees. It was to keep employees from spending time

GOOGLE DOODLES

In 1999, the Google logo appeared on users' computers with a stick figure in the second *o*. Staff members were on their way to the annual Burning Man festival, where the highlight is the burning of a large, wooden, human-shaped structure. The logo change was the first of what came to be called Google Doodles. Now a committee is in charge of these temporary changes to the Google logo on the search site. They often commemorate birthdays of notable individuals, as well as events such as Earth Day, International Women's Day, and the Olympics. The Doodles sometimes vary internationally, with specific images appearing only in certain countries.

Food served at work is one of several perks Google offers to make working for the company more attractive.

going out to get food. That was time they could have spent working. One former employee said Google was like a "velvet prison," meaning that while it is made of very nice material, you're still stuck inside. Engineers tend to work longer hours at Google than at a regular office job. As the former employee explained, "Twelve hours a day, six days a week was typical."[3] That's far above the eight hours per day, five days per week that many office workers expect to work.

For some Googlers, the pressure of this company culture is too much, but for others, it is a great opportunity. One popular benefit is the company's policy of "20 percent time." All engineers are encouraged to use

20 percent of their time, or about one day per workweek, on a project that interests them, rather than on assigned work. Some Googlers have used this 20 percent time to develop new initiatives and services for the company. This program makes some people feel good about their jobs because they get to do things they really want to do. Other Googlers find it hard to use their 20 percent time because they're so busy doing their required work.

FINDING MONEY

But culture wasn't the only issue in Google's early years. First, Google needed money. Ram Shriram offered to help. Shriram, a friend of Page and Brin, had worked for early internet companies, including Netscape Communications and Amazon. He became one of Google's first angel investors. This type of investor

GOOGLE NEWS

On September 11, 2001, terrorists hijacked four airplanes in the United States. Three planes were deliberately crashed into buildings, and one crashed in a field after the passengers fought back. As the attack unfolded, all planes flying over or to the United States were immediately grounded. Krishna Bharat, a Google employee stranded in New Orleans, Louisiana, was frustrated trying to learn what was happening. News stories changed quickly, and many websites couldn't link to articles fast enough for Google searches to work well. As his 20 percent project, Bharat developed new algorithms that used the general reputations of news outlets, not just web traffic, to rank their articles. The resulting search product, Google News, searches specifically among news sources, rather than looking at the entire web.

gives money to a new company without necessarily expecting to profit from the investment. However, if the company happens to strike it rich, the investor can profit significantly. Shriram also suggested Page and Brin meet with Andy Bechtolsheim, who had cofounded the major tech company Sun Microsystems. Bechtolsheim visited their office and liked what Brin and Page were doing. He left them a check for $100,000 made out to Google, Inc.[4] When Page and Brin told Bechtolsheim they didn't have a company bank account yet, he told them to keep the check until they did. Within the next few months, David Cheriton, a computer science professor at Stanford, and Jeff Bezos, founder and chief executive officer (CEO) of Amazon, also became angel investors for the fledgling Google. But this money wouldn't last forever.

Menlo Park, California, was a good place for new technology companies partly

DON'T BE EVIL

In 2001, Google executives, without Page and Brin, met to try to establish company ideals. They came up with a list, but one phrase seemed to cover all of them: "Don't be evil."[5] Famously, this became the motto of the corporation. Although the motto was intended to help guide Googlers and to reassure the public, it has sometimes backfired for Google. What exactly "evil" means, critics point out, is often defined by only Page and Brin. Over the years, critics pointed to the company's advertising, its use of personal information, and its business dealings to say that Google doesn't always live up to this motto.

because there were so many venture capital firms nearby. Venture capital firms make a business of investing in new companies. Essentially, they bet on new ideas. Many of the companies they invest in fail. But the ones that succeed, such as Google, often make so much money that the firm has no problem staying in business.

But Page and Brin worried that a venture capital firm would make decisions for Google. Their solution was to look for two firms and ask each to provide half of the $25 million they needed. In 1999, Sequoia Capital and Kleiner Perkins each agreed to invest $12.5 million in Google on the condition that Page and Brin hire a CEO who was experienced in business.[6] After all, Google's founders were still fresh from graduate school.

ONLINE INFRASTRUCTURE

The years 1998 and 1999 were a relatively good time for Google to be looking for investors. When the internet and the World Wide Web became widely available in the 1990s, it was expected that the technology industry would keep growing at breakneck speed. Many new internet-based companies took off and made millions, and plenty of people were willing to invest in what was expected to be the next big thing. The problems came around 2000, with what is called the dot-com bust. Although more and more people used the internet every year, the industry's growth wasn't as huge as some people had expected. As confidence dropped, so did funding and sales, and a lot of new internet (or *dot-com*) companies went out of business. For the companies that remained, including Google, this actually meant an opportunity to grow.

Some of those companies had installed fiber-optic cables underground before they went out of business. These cables are very thin strands of glass that use laser light to move a lot of data at high speed. They transfer data dramatically faster than the standard phone lines that had been used before. They can provide internet access to individual houses in a neighborhood, or they can run between and across continents or under oceans. Google started buying up fiber-optic lines that had been installed and never used. Owning its own cables meant that Google could move data from one end of the country to the other basically for free.

Google also saw opportunity in data centers. It is common practice for many tech companies, and particularly internet-based companies, to keep large numbers of their servers in these specially constructed

Data centers are filled with rows upon rows of computers that support a company's internet infrastructure.

buildings. Keeping them in a central location makes them easier to maintain and manage. Like any computer, the harder these machines work, the more heat they produce. The hotter it gets, the harder they have to work to accomplish the same things. So, ventilation and cooling are very important in data centers. A company's servers are often kept in chain-link cages inside the data center. This allows air to flow freely around the computers while keeping them protected from unauthorized access. In 2000, many server buildings had space to rent for cheap because their clients no longer existed. Google's constantly expanding number of servers meant it rented out more and more space in these buildings. Eventually, Google was renting not just sections, but entire buildings for its servers.

Page and Brin eventually set out to have their own server buildings constructed. Working in secrecy, they set up everything to construct their first data centers in The Dalles, Oregon, in 2006. The town had its own hydroelectric power source, as well as a fiber-optic network for transferring data to and from the center.

By 2018, Google had 15 data centers around the world.[7] Each requires a great deal of energy. In 2005, one

Google's data centers in The Dalles, Oregon, are enormous facilities.

study estimated that data centers overall used 1.2 percent
of all power in the United States. This was twice the
amount from 2000, and more than the amount used by
the populations of some entire states. Google, with all its
data centers, was one of the largest single energy users.
Google is as secretive about its data centers as it is about
much of the rest of its business, so exact statistics about
the company's energy use aren't known. But in 2017,
the company announced it relied entirely on renewable
energy for all of its global operations.

CHAPTER FOUR

DRAMATIC EXPANSION

Page and Brin had some interest from investors, but they still lacked a business plan. They had no idea how Google would earn money, but they were sure about one thing: they hated the idea of advertising on their search engine. To this day, Google's home page is mostly white space. It is valuable space that could be sold to advertisers, but Page and Brin refuse.

Other search companies allowed advertisers to pay to have their websites listed higher in the search results. But Page felt that "any time you accept money to influence the results, even if it is just for inclusion, it is probably a bad thing."[1] Additionally, when Google first started, many users still relied on dial-up internet connections. Data ran through regular phone lines. Pages could take a long time to load, especially if they had images. Page and Brin didn't want to slow

Gmail is one of several products and services that Google introduced as it underwent significant growth in the early 2000s.

down the load time. Instead, Page and Brin decided, Google would make money from companies willing to pay to use their search technology.

Google put this plan to the test in partnership with Netscape, the company behind one of the top web browsers of the time. At that time, Netscape was owned by the huge internet service provider America Online (AOL). In 1999, Google became the default search provider for Netscape. On the first day, Google's servers were so overloaded that its own website was shut down briefly. The Google engineers learned to plan bigger. By autumn 1999, Google handled 3.5 million searches a day.[2] In 2000, the company signed a contract to handle search traffic from Yahoo! too. Google's search volume doubled on the first day. Most users didn't know they were getting Google's search results because Google's name wasn't on the page. But Google was getting valuable data about how its search engine was working.

In 2001, Google hired an outsider to help lead the company. Eric Schmidt joined the company's board before becoming CEO. A veteran of the technology industry, Schmidt would provide the business knowledge to help shepherd Google through its period of rapid growth.

ERIC SCHMIDT

Eric Schmidt grew up in Virginia. He came from an academic household like both Brin and Page. Schmidt's father was a professor of economics at Johns Hopkins University and at Virginia Tech, and his mother held a master's degree in psychology. When he was in grade school, Schmidt became fascinated by early computers, which could run only one or two programs at a time. A system called time-sharing allowed multiple users to run programs on a single central computer, using slices of time.

Schmidt studied electrical engineering at Princeton University and earned a master's and PhD in computer engineering from the University of California, Berkeley. After graduating, he worked at Xerox's Palo Alto Research Center. This groundbreaking lab produced technologies that would be crucial to the internet and personal computers. Later, he worked for Sun Microsystems and eventually became CEO of Novell, both major technology companies.

When Schmidt first met Brin and Page, "we argued for at least 90 minutes," says Schmidt.[3] Although Google's founders didn't want to hire a CEO, they liked Schmidt. He was experienced and educated in both computers and business management. Schmidt served as Google CEO from 2001 to 2011, when he became chairman of the board of directors for Google. Larry Page became CEO in his place. In 2018, Schmidt stepped down as chairman as well, remaining with Alphabet only as a technical adviser.

Schmidt brought business management skills to Google.

ADVERTISING

In the end, it was advertising that allowed Google to hit it big. But ads on Google worked differently than those on other search engines. It started with a program called AdWords, which allowed people or companies to purchase certain key words. When a user searched for those words through Google, up to three advertisements would be displayed in a separate column to the side of the search results. These ads were text only, so no images would slow down the page's load time. Only 15 percent of search queries, those involving relevant keywords, returned ads alongside search results. AdWords launched in 2000. Advertisers paid Google based on the number of people who saw their ads.

In 2002, Google changed its advertising system in a big way. Now, advertisers paid based on the number of people who clicked on their ads, not how many times they were displayed. This is called cost-per-click or pay-per-click. If an ad didn't work, it might not cost an advertiser anything. If it was successful, it would make money for the advertiser and Google.

That year, Google won several more major contracts. In the spring, Google agreed to provide search and ads for AOL's web portal. Google paid AOL millions of dollars for the privilege, but the two companies shared the advertising revenue. It also partnered with internet service provider EarthLink, and it even worked with competitor Ask Jeeves.

A few years later, Google bought DoubleClick, a company that provided banner advertising. Banners are images, and sometimes videos, that run at the top or side of a web page. Google was already the biggest company in search advertising. With the purchase of DoubleClick, Google gained control of internet advertising in general. Competitors claimed that Google had become a monopoly—a single company unfairly controlling an entire market. Then and now, most of Google's money comes from advertising. By 2018, Google would control just under one-half of the US digital advertising market.[4]

GOING PUBLIC

But back in 2004, Page and Brin had higher hopes. Advertising income wasn't enough to reach their lofty goals. Money from investors was running out. They needed more funds.

One way for a company to raise a lot of money is to allow individuals to buy small portions, called shares or stock, in a company. When a company begins to sell shares, the process is called going public. The first time a company offers to sell stock is called the initial public offering (IPO). And IPOs require a lot of paperwork beforehand. The company must publish how much money it is making and spending every year. That gives investors information to help them decide whether to purchase shares.

Google had been a private company for seven years. Page and Brin had kept company revenues private. Most people still thought internet search didn't make money. Google liked it that way. If nobody knew how much money Google was making, Page and Brin didn't have to worry too much about competition. As a result of the IPO, the world learned in 2004 that Google had been profitable for the last three years. Not only that,

GOOGLE GLOBAL REVENUE, 2002-2017 (BILLIONS OF DOLLARS)[5]

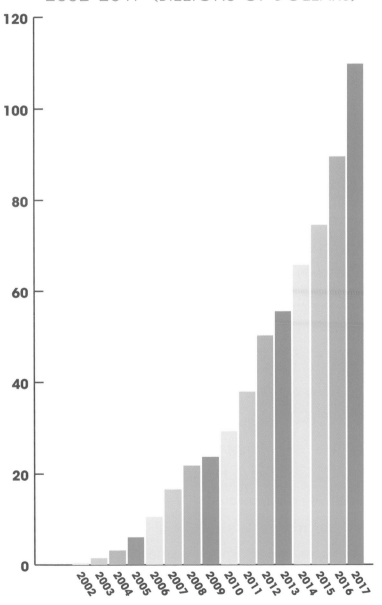

but Google had brought in $64 million of profit (out of $389 million revenue) in the first three months of 2004.[6]

When Google's stock first went on sale, the company raised $1.67 billion.[7] That was more than any other technology company had ever made in its IPO. Suddenly, Google had an enormous influx of cash to fuel its continued expansion.

GMAIL

In the same year as its IPO, Google introduced a new service for users: Gmail. This free email service offered users 250 times as much storage as other major providers.[8] Suddenly users didn't have to delete emails to make space.

What was Google getting out of it? The data would be stored on Google's servers rather than the user's computer. That made people wonder what Google was going to do with that personal information. Also, critics worried, the company's servers could be hacked and personal information could be stolen. And Gmail included advertisements that were targeted based on keywords found in users' emails. People worried that Google was reading private communication, despite Page and Brin promising that it was all done by computer. Google analyzes users' data in order to target ads to them. The more emails you keep, the more Google knows about how to target ads toward you—and the more money Google and its advertisers can make. Gmail became popular with users, turning into one of the top five email services in the world.

ANDROID

Around the same time, Page and Brin were realizing that mobile devices could someday eclipse desktop and laptop computers. They needed to make sure Google was ready for this shift in the technology industry. So, in 2005, Google bought the secretive company Android. It created software for mobile phones, though the public knew little about what it was working on.

In June 2007, the introduction of Apple's

ANDY RUBIN

Andy Rubin worked at many tech companies, including Apple and Microsoft. Danger, Inc., a company he formed, designed the T-Mobile Sidekick, an early smartphone with text messaging and internet capability. Rubin cofounded Android in 2003. Page and Brin were fans of the Sidekick, and they were sure mobile devices would play an important part in Google's future. Since Rubin left Google in 2014, he's started Playground, a company that helps start-ups through engineering and financing. He also created Essential, a hardware company that released its first smartphone in 2017.

iPhone revolutionized the mobile phone industry. The smartphone replaced the physical keypads of older phones with a giant touch screen. Android's designers worked to match what Apple had done. Later that year, Google announced that Android would be a smartphone operating system. It would provide the operating system to mobile phone manufacturers for free, encouraging the rapid growth of Android. The company would soon be in competition with Apple in the smartphone industry.

The iPhone came with Google as the default search tool. It also used Google Maps for its mapping data, and it had a special version of YouTube. At Google, in the same building that Android's engineers were developing their own mobile platform, a department worked to make Google services compatible with the iPhone. Page and Brin both used iPhones and were good friends with Apple CEO Steve Jobs. Andy Rubin, cofounder of Android and head of the Android division within Google at that time, wasn't sure his department had the support of his bosses. At one point, a colleague heard Rubin tell Brin, "We have to stop giving our best stuff away to Apple if we want Android to succeed."[9]

The first Android phone, the G1, was not successful.

Sure enough, in 2008, tensions between Apple and Google came to a head. Executives of the companies held a meeting in which people became very confrontational. From then on, Google put all of its energies behind Android and distanced itself from Apple.

When the first Android phone was released in late 2008, it did not find widespread popularity. Its touch screen technology was lacking compared with that of the iPhone. Its failure motivated Google to push harder to rival Apple.

Mobile phone manufacturers were eager to work with Google to challenge Apple. The phone provider Verizon would carry a Motorola-made iPhone rival with an Android operating system. The new phone, called the Droid, launched in 2009. It was advertised as a direct competitor to the iPhone. In its first three months, it outsold the original iPhone. It was followed by the Nexus One, which had a bigger screen and a better camera than the iPhone, as well as touch screen technology to rival the Apple device.

Android's fleet of phones continued to expand. In 2010 alone, the platform increased from seven million users to 67 million.[10] Google partners were selling 200,000 cell phones a day.[11] By 2017, Android was running on about eight of every ten mobile phones in the world.[12] After ten years of competition with the iPhone, Google more than caught up.

YOUTUBE

Using some of the cash from its IPO, Google bought YouTube for $1.65 billion in 2006.[13] Video, Google was sure, would be another important portion of the world's information that needed cataloging. In more practical terms, getting into the online video market meant a

lot more advertising. People
spend about one billion
hours combined every
day on YouTube, watching
videos displayed alongside
advertisements or sometimes
preceded by advertisements.

Owning YouTube also
exposed Google to a number
of complaints and even legal
issues. Individual users can
upload anything to the site.
Sometimes the videos or
accompanying information
might be offensive, though the exact definition of
offensive and the way YouTube has applied this policy
have been the subject of intense debate. Users might also
upload copyrighted material to YouTube. According to the
Online Copyright Infringement Liability Limitation Act of
1997, the company is required to remove anything that's
under copyright protection. The company developed
tools to automatically detect songs and other copyrighted
material in uploaded videos.

YOUTUBE IS BORN

In 2005, three engineers who had worked for the online payment company PayPal founded YouTube. With viral videos spreading throughout the web, founder Jawed Karim saw the opportunity for a site that made it easy for users to find, watch, and share videos. Unable to find investors, the team used its own money to create the site. Within a year and a half of its creation, YouTube had 34 million visitors every month.[14]

CHAPTER **FIVE**

GOOGLE AROUND THE WORLD

G oogle's goal is to make information available to the world. But information is useless unless it can be understood, and most of the world doesn't speak English. In 2000, Google began to offer search in ten European languages, including Italian, French, and Norwegian.

By 2004, Google finally had international engineering offices. One was in Zurich, Switzerland. Two were in Israel, in the cities of Tel Aviv and Haifa. Krishna Bharat, who had developed Google News, volunteered to head the company's offices in India. By 2018, Google had offices in 25 cities in North America and more than 40 other cities around the world. Its search page is offered in more than 120 languages.

Cataloging information in languages other than English was critical to Google's mission.

FOLLOWING THE RULES

Google must follow the laws and customs of the countries in which it works. Many countries have asked Google to censor its search results and YouTube videos. In Thailand, for example, it is illegal to insult the king. Google's deputy general counsel visited the country and concluded that it was appropriate for Google to block Thai users from seeing videos that insult the king. In France and Germany, it is illegal to deny the Holocaust or to spread what those countries define as hate speech. In those countries, Google blocks any search results that do so.

On the other hand, in 2008, Turkey requested that Google block all users around the world from seeing YouTube videos that insulted the founder of modern Turkey. Google agreed to block those videos within Turkey. But the company refused to block the videos for all other countries. In response, Turkey's government blocked access to all of YouTube within the country.

CHINA

Google's work in China was the most challenging. Google worked on a Chinese version of its search engine starting in 2000. But it wasn't until 2006 that Google opened

Internet users in Turkey found themselves unable to access YouTube in 2008. Many people protested this and other heavy-handed government censorship actions.

an office in China. The Chinese government insisted on controlling what information its citizens could access. China wanted Google to agree to block information from its search results in China. If it didn't agree, the government would prevent Google from operating there at all. Google decided that it could do more good for freedom of information by working in China, even if results were censored. So the company hired Kai-Fu Lee to head the new office.

Lee walked a narrow path of compromise between the Chinese government, which wanted censorship, and Google, which wanted freedom of information. But there were some things the company would not offer in China. If Chinese officials believed a person was acting or speaking out against the government, that person could be imprisoned. To find these people, the government might ask Google for information on its users. Google did not want to give it to them. So, Google would not store anyone's personal data within China. If the company did, China could demand the information against Google's will. That meant that services such as Gmail and Blogger were not available for users in China. And the Chinese government blocked access to YouTube.

In 2006, Google.cn, the company's China-based search page, launched. Unfortunately for Google, most internet users in China already had a favorite search engine: Baidu.

Developed by Robin Li, Baidu became popular almost instantly after its launch in 2001. It functioned differently than Google in several ways. It mixed paid advertisements with search results. As a company, Baidu gave names of political activists to the Chinese government. And although Li was hesitant to follow a government order to censor results, he did agree, saying, "It's just Chinese law. I'm not in politics. I'm not in a position to judge what's right and wrong."[2] So before Google.cn went live, Baidu had already secured more than one-half of the search market in China.[3] Google, several years behind Baidu, never managed to overtake it.

CENSORING THE WEB

To keep its operating license in China, Google had to agree to block some search results. Page and Brin weren't happy, but it was the cost of doing business there. As a compromise, the bottom of the search results page listed how many results were blocked. According to critics, Google.cn was "scary-good" at blocking information the government didn't want Chinese citizens to access. This included images of a famous 1989 protest for democracy in which protesters in Beijing's Tiananmen Square suffered

Baidu eventually became one of the largest tech companies in China.

from a police crackdown. It also included any websites about opponents or critics of the Chinese government.

According to Lee, not all of China's people saw censorship as a problem. Some of the company's Chinese engineers didn't realize that blocking some search results was controversial until Lee discussed it with them. Some people living in China, though, knew that they couldn't see the same information as others in the world saw. It bothered them greatly to have the government decide for them what they could view.

STRAINED RELATIONS WITH CHINA

In 2008, the Chinese government made another demand of Google. Google.cn was just for China. But people in China could also go to Google.com, the international page, and translate it into Chinese. Even though some of those results were blocked by the Chinese government, people could still find more search results that way. Even some Chinese officials used the international search page to see what the world was saying about them—information that might be blocked because it criticized the government. So China asked Google to block certain information from the Chinese-language version of Google.com. Google executives refused. The company's relationship with the Chinese government became tenser.

In 2009, only three years after Google's China office first opened, the security team in the home office discovered the company's main database had been hacked. The attack had originated in China. This was the last straw. The company announced it would no longer censor search results. Google even said that if it had to, it would close down Google.cn or close its office in China. The engineers in the China office had not been warned. They were surprised by the announcement. Google executives tried to negotiate with the Chinese

GOOGLE TRANSLATE

Scientists have been working since at least the 1950s to develop a machine that can translate languages. Beginning in 2003, Google engineers used United Nations (UN) documents and Google News stories to teach their computer programs billions of words in many languages. In 2007, a trial version of Google Translate launched. It offered English translations of Russian, Chinese, and Arabic texts. By the following summer, Google was able to translate text between more than 20 languages, including Spanish, Korean, Finnish, and Hindi.

In 2016, Google announced a new version. This newer Google Translate used technology known as deep learning. The translation software improves over time as it does more translations. It vastly improved the quality of Translate's results. Some critics worry that machine translations will leave human translators out of work. But many experts agree there is an art to human language and translation that computers, at least for now, can't recreate.

government, but the two sides couldn't agree. Beginning in 2010, users who went to Google.cn were rerouted to Google.hk—the search page for Hong Kong. This page was outside the reach of China's censors. Some information would still be blocked for users in China, but it wasn't Google doing the blocking.

In 2018, Chinese users were suddenly able to access the previously blocked websites for Google Translate and Google Maps. Google Search was still blocked. Because of legal restrictions, the Google Maps service did not actually work in China—it just linked to a map service by Alibaba, a China-based search company. In 2017, Google announced its plans to open another office

In this cartoon posted at an internet café in China, a policeman says, "Please come with me because you published materials to harm the unity of the nation."

in the country, focused on engineering. In particular, the company wants to take part in the booming artificial intelligence (AI) market. When she announced the new AI lab, Google AI scientist Fei-Fei Li said, "I believe AI and its benefits have no borders. Whether a breakthrough occurs in Silicon Valley, Beijing or anywhere else, it has the potential to make everyone's life better for the entire world."[4] The lab will be one of five Google labs around the world focused specifically on AI.

CHAPTER **SIX**

GOOGLE AND THE GOVERNMENT

I n 2010, Google announced that it had been hacked. Its security team had traced the attack to a server in Taiwan. The team believed, and said publicly, that the hackers were supported by the Chinese government. Security researchers discovered that more than 20 companies had been hacked in related attacks. They included Yahoo!, software company Adobe, and the defense contractor Northrop Grumman. The total number of affected companies later rose to more than 30.[1] "We have never ever, outside of the defense industry, seen commercial industrial companies come under that level of sophisticated attack," said one researcher. "It's totally changing the threat model."[2]

Google's operations in China were hampered by political events and government-sponsored hacking.

The hackers stole secret information about Google's products and services. They also tried to break into the email accounts of human rights activists, who are often targeted by the Chinese government. When Google disclosed the hack, it became the first US company to announce a security breach that came from China. China is a large and growing market. Tech companies often try to avoid annoying its government. But Google was already compromising by agreeing to censor material for users in China. After the hack, Google had had enough. It announced it would no longer censor search results in China. It said it would even shut down its main Chinese search page if necessary. Google's stand raised questions for the rest of the tech industry. Would other American companies accept China's suppression of free speech in order to make money there?

Google's announcement shook its presence in China. But it also created an opportunity for the US government. Several firms, including Google, had been asking US government officials to help stop Chinese cyberattacks and piracy. But President Barack Obama and other officials were unwilling to say anything unless there was solid proof that it was happening. Accusing China without proof would simply harm the US–China relationship.

So, instead of waiting for the US government to start the discussion, Google started it. Following Google's announcement, Secretary of State Hillary Clinton asked China's government to answer for these cyberattacks. It wasn't the US government claiming China illegally hacked American companies—it was Google. In 2018, under President Donald Trump, the US government began more forcefully challenging the Chinese government over the hacking of Google and other US companies.

WHY WOULD CHINA HACK AMERICAN COMPANIES?

Google believed that the hackers were looking for information about people who oppose the Chinese government. According to Google's blog post about the attack, the hackers failed in this. The same post said that many Gmail accounts of political activists around the world had been broken into. As Google learned more, it looked like the Chinese hackers were searching for information about people the FBI might be following. It is thought the hackers were searching for evidence about whether the United States had discovered any Chinese spies.

COOPERATION AND LOBBYING

The aftermath of the hack was not the first time Google worked alongside the US government. In 2005, Hurricane Katrina hit the Gulf Coast. Google Maps was only a few months old, but for many people, it was a vital tool. Residents who fled the storm used Maps and its photographic overlay, Google Earth, to assess the damage to their homes and neighborhoods. People across the United States helped overlay aerial images from the National Oceanic and Atmospheric Administration (NOAA) onto Google's view. Within a few days, Google and NOAA joined forces to make a "Katrina view" on Maps to share this information. In October 2012, Hurricane Sandy barreled over New Jersey and New York. Google's Crisis Response team created a map of fuel inventories, power outages, and road repairs. Volunteer groups used Maps to let people know where there was a need for extra supplies or man power.

Google has worked to influence the public on internet policy issues. In 2012, the Stop Online Piracy Act, a bill on the floor of the US Congress, threatened to limit access to websites that host or help users to access pirated content, such as music or movies. That meant that YouTube could potentially get in trouble. The same thing applied to search engines like Google, which could lead users to such pirated content. Google added links to its search page that encouraged users to write to their congresspeople to vote against the act. Within days, the proposed bill was withdrawn.

After the 2016 US presidential election, there was evidence that people working for the Russian government tried to influence American voters by buying misleading or false advertisements online. US law bans foreign groups or governments from campaigning for or against American candidates. In 2017 and 2018, Congress called executives from tech companies to testify. Most of the information Congress reviewed was on the social networking site Facebook. But several thousand ads were placed through Google. Google suggested that the law should prohibit foreign entities from advertising on issues and candidates. Also, the laws don't specify that they apply to

GOOGLE AND ANTITRUST LAWS

Antitrust laws prevent businesses from taking unfair advantage over competitors. More than once, the US government has had to rule whether Google was violating these laws. The Federal Trade Commission spent most of a year examining Google's 2007 purchase of DoubleClick. Google already controlled the majority of search advertising. Google's defense was that it sold ads, while DoubleClick only decided where best to place them. The sale went through.

The next year, Microsoft offered to buy Yahoo!. Google offered to make a deal to show some of its own ads on Yahoo! search results. That way, Yahoo! would get a cut of the advertising money, and it would be able to stay independent. Microsoft accused Google of forming a monopoly with Yahoo!, creating an unfair advantage against Microsoft. The company lobbied for the Justice Department to bring an antitrust case against Google. Google soon dropped the deal with Yahoo!.

Officials from Facebook, *left*, Twitter, *center*, and Google, *right*, testified in front of Congress in October 2017.

online advertising. Google proposed that restrictions on political ads be clearer.

Google has also engaged in lobbying, working to persuade the government to act in a particular way. From 2013 to 2017, Google spent about $15 million every year on lobbying.[3] It may be the biggest spender in tech. But Apple, Amazon, Facebook, and Microsoft also spend millions of dollars every year to influence the government. Often, these competing companies are on the same side of policy issues. For example, the tech industry has been very supportive of immigration. If talented foreigners enter the United States to work or study, then companies like Google can widen their hiring pools. In 2017, the administration of President Trump threatened to revoke a law allowing spouses of highly skilled workers to get jobs in the United States. Technology companies and their employees were loudly opposed. They supported the law.

NET NEUTRALITY

Another key internet issue of interest to Google is net neutrality. This is the idea that all online content should be treated equally by internet service providers, such as the telecom company Verizon. Under net neutrality, these providers are not allowed to slow down or block certain websites or people's access to those websites. Without net neutrality, the worry is that providers could create an

PATENTS AND LAWSUITS

Patents are licenses granted by the government to protect inventors. For a set period of time, only the patent holder can profit from the invention. Sometimes even tiny parts of a complex invention, such as a smartphone, are patented. This allows the patent holders to demand payment when others use the patents.

Patent infringement lawsuits are very common in the technology industry. In 2009, software company Oracle sued Google. Oracle said that Android copied code owned by Sun Microsystems, a company Oracle had recently bought. In 2010, Apple and Microsoft sued some of the companies that made Android phones, but not Google itself. In 2011, Google bought 17,000 patents from Motorola's mobile division.[4] This meant that when other companies threatened to sue, Google could either make a deal with them or threaten to sue back.

unfair playing field, slowing down service for certain companies or charging users extra to access certain sites.

In 2015, the Federal Communications Commission (FCC) voted to strengthen net neutrality rules. Then in 2017, new leadership of the FCC under President Trump repealed these rules. The FCC said the rules prevented companies from testing different business models and pricing plans. Net neutrality supporters worried that without guaranteed equal access to the internet, the ability of small businesses to make a profit could be stifled.

Opposition to the 2017 repeal was strong. State and federal lawmakers almost immediately discussed replacing net neutrality laws. The governors of Montana and New York issued executive orders to require net neutrality in their respective states. In March 2018, the state of Washington passed a law prohibiting internet providers from blocking or slowing content in that state. But state rules like this were explicitly prohibited by the FCC's ruling. The FCC says that providers cross state lines, so only the FCC has authority over them. Nevertheless, several state attorneys general promised to bring the FCC to court, as did a handful of organizations.

As one of the internet's most-used services, Google has a large stake in net neutrality. In 2006, Brin flew to Washington, DC, to argue in favor of net neutrality. Yet the company mostly stayed out of the spotlight before the 2017 FCC vote. The company was heavily criticized for this. In 2017, Google joined several other technology companies in encouraging the public to voice their opinions to the FCC. Shortly after net neutrality was removed, the

YOUNG PEOPLE FIGHT FOR NET NEUTRALITY

Teenagers were particularly vocal in support of net neutrality, both before and after the 2017 FCC vote. About 94 percent of Americans age 13 to 17 use social media and the internet multiple times a day.[6] Students took part in text and phone campaigns, protested and marched, and contacted their legislators.

Internet users across the United States have protested in favor of net neutrality.

Industry Association, a collection of companies including Google, Facebook, and Netflix, announced it would join legal actions against the FCC to restore the policy.

Google's income and the company ideals are wrapped up in making the web open and available to everyone. It recommitted to that goal in its dealings in China. Industry experts continue to watch Google to see whether it will put its money and power where it says its values are.

CHAPTER SEVEN

INVESTING IN SOCIETY

I n Google's early years, Page planned to put all the books in the world online. The result of this desire was Google Books. Page had worked on a digital library project before Google Books. Stanford University's Digital Library Project was a framework for publishers to upload publications. And before Google Books, Google had experimented in digitizing catalogs. Merchants volunteered for their catalogs to be searchable, on a separate database from a regular Google search. Not many signed up, and eventually Catalog Search was abandoned.

SCANNING BOOKS

In 2002, Page recruited Google employee Marissa Mayer to help him photograph an entire book. Using a camera on a tripod and a metronome to keep their pace, Page and Mayer photographed

Devices that scan books rapidly were key to the success of Google Books.

DIGITAL LIBRARY PROJECTS

Digital library projects have existed in various forms for decades. Project Gutenberg started in 1971, before computers and image scanners were readily available. Individual volunteers copied the text of books in the public domain. When the World Wide Web was created, Project Gutenberg expanded its call for typists. By 2002, the project had digitized the text of 6,300 works.[3]

Carnegie Mellon University started the Million Book Project in 2001. The scanning was done in India and China, where costs were lower. When the project ended in 2007, it had scanned 1.4 million books, most of them in Chinese, Hindi, and other languages, loaned from the countries where the scanning was being done.[4]

every page of a 300-page book. Company legend says that they were then able to calculate how long it would take to digitize all the world's books. Schmidt later said they estimated there were more than 129 million separate book titles in the world.[1] Google set a timeline of ten years to digitize the entire world's collection of books. Mayer called it a "moon shot" because it was such a large project, like the US goal in the 1960s of landing humans on the moon.[2]

The biggest challenge with Page's idea was copyright. Copyright protects the creators of an original work and sometimes their heirs. Others cannot use the material without permission and often payment. Some material, mostly that on which copyright has expired, is not protected by copyright laws. It is said to be in the public domain. But Google wanted to scan all books, not just public domain ones. Making an entire copyrighted work available to the public without permission from the copyright owner is illegal. One exception to copyright law is the notion of fair use. This allows for the free use of small excerpts of copyrighted works for education, criticism, or other purposes.

Google intended to index the information in each publication but not allow users to read whole books for free. Users would be able to search books to see if they contained information they wanted, but they would be limited in how much of the book they could view. Google's efforts weren't a clear copyright violation, but they also weren't clearly allowed. The company found itself in a legal gray area. Some authors and publishers began to object loudly.

In 2005, Google announced partnerships in its program. The New York Public Library, the Bodleian Library at Oxford University, and several university libraries in the United States agreed to let Google scan their books. At first, Google didn't mention that each of these libraries limited which books would be scanned. One exception was the University of Michigan, which allowed Google to digitize all its books. Google also didn't

Stanford University was among the partners that allowed Google to scan its library collections.

say what the company intended to do about all the books still under copyright.

That year, the Authors Guild, a professional organization for writers, sued Google for copyright infringement. The judge in the case found that Google Book Search provided a "significant public benefit."[5] Because it worked like an online card catalog, circuit court justices said that it "tests the boundaries of fair use" but doesn't cross them.[6] The case went through an appeals process, but ten years later, in 2015, it was dismissed.

By 2007, Yahoo! and Microsoft were also beginning digitizing efforts. By then, Google had scanned about one million books.[7] One adjustment that year helped boost the numbers. Using titles, authors, and publication dates, Google added listings for millions of books to its catalog before they'd been scanned. These listings also included online reviews of the publication, lists of links from around the web, and citations from other books already scanned. Depending on the agreement Google had made with a book's publisher, the book might appear with all its pages, just a few of them, or none at all.

CHROMEBOOKS

Google's Chromebook, a basic laptop built around its Chrome web browser, is very popular in some schools. It is cheaper than Apple's iPad tablet, making it more accessible to schools with limited budgets. In 2016, Chromebooks

THE OPEN CONTENT ALLIANCE

Google Books was a popular idea, but some people disliked the fact that the volumes would be available only through Google. In 2005, several organizations formed the Open Content Alliance (OCA). The OCA would digitize books and make them available to all search engines and libraries.

Yahoo! was a leader in the organization. The National Archive of Britain and several universities joined the OCA early on. Some research libraries that had rejected contracts with Google chose to work with the OCA. Within two years, the OCA had scanned 100,000 books.[8]

In 2008, Microsoft, the main financial supporter of the alliance, stopped development of its book searching service. It also withdrew from the OCA. Without more funding, the OCA was unable to continue digitizing. In 2018, its digital files were still accessible online and through multiple libraries.

made up nearly one-half of all computer devices purchased for education. They sync with the Google Cloud, a system that stores files on remote computers that are accessible through the internet from any device. That can be a helpful feature for users, and it is good for Google because it also keeps people using only Google's services. Another benefit is that multiple students can use the same Chromebook and keep their information private because Chromebooks require signing in with a Google account. This is also useful, though it requires everyone to have or create a Google account.

The devices are used mostly in wealthier schools in the United States. Much of the developing world lacks the high-speed internet needed to make Chromebooks useful,

Many schools provide Chromebooks for their students to use.

though Google is also working on projects to improve global internet access. And in China, home to more than 1.4 billion of the world's 7.6 billion people, many Google apps are inaccessible.[9]

Google isn't providing educational services for classrooms just to be nice. The company has access to a great deal of sensitive information from all these users. Privacy concerns have been a consistent complaint against Google, but using data belonging to school children has been seen as particularly worrisome. Its education apps do not include ads, but information was gathered that allowed Google to place ads elsewhere on students' Google accounts. In 2013, students filed a lawsuit against Google for collecting their information. In response, the company said it would stop gathering such data from its education applications. Still, in 2015, the nonprofit Electronic Frontier Foundation accused Google of doing just that. Google denied the accusation.

GOOGLE.ORG

Google is a business. It is interested in profit. But it also has a long-standing interest in philanthropic, or charitable, goals. Google's charity work is done by a part of the company known as Google.org. It is sometimes simply called DotOrg. Beginning in 2003, Google has offered free advertising space to organizations it believed would benefit society. In Page's 2004 letter to potential investors, he promised 1 percent of Google's profits would go to supporting nonprofits.

In 2005, Google announced a new program to provide funding and volunteers from Google to help certain charities. Google would tackle issues such as sustainable energy, climate change, poverty, and disease. It would also use some funding to lobby for changes to public policy and to support companies that Google's executives believe support social progress. The company gave Google.org three million shares of Google stock.[10] It has millions of dollars of funding to dispense every year.

Few experts would deny that education around the world could use financial help. By some estimates, 264 million of the world's children do not go to school.[11] Google has donated funds and employee time to organizations around the world to help fix that.

Since 2007, Google has worked with Pratham Education Foundation in India. The company supports Pratham's Hybrid Learning Program, which provides technology for students to share and learn together.

It also supports Pratham Books, a not-for-profit publisher. Pratham has translated hundreds of books into 18 different languages, helping students throughout India learn to read, and it has lowered the cost of books.[12]

Google also funds many other organizations and projects around the world. Some of their goals include improving accessibility for people with disabilities, providing job training and placement for the disabled and for veterans, and bringing more women and girls into information technology. One program, Code.org, seeks to make computer science education more common in schools. Another, the California-based Khan Academy, offers free online classes to people of any age around the world. Google also helped fund several US education organizations. They offer opportunities to students of color and to children living in poverty.

KHAN ACADEMY AND CRAIG SILVERSTEIN

Craig Silverstein was hired in 1998 as the first employee of Google after Brin and Page. A fellow Stanford student along with the founders, Silverstein cowrote several papers with Brin. In 2012, he left Google to become a developer for Khan Academy. Khan Academy offers free online classes in math, science, arts and the humanities, computer science and engineering, and test prep. When he moved to Khan Academy, Silverstein brought with him his practice of baking bread in the office to share with everyone. His new coworkers were thrilled.

Since 2013, Google.org has held what it calls impact challenge contests. The public and a company panel vote for which organizations will receive Google funding and engineering support. Winners have tackled problems in education, the environment, interaction with government, medicine and sanitation, and accessibility. In 2017, Google.org announced it would issue $1 billion in grants and up to one million volunteer hours to nonprofits that worked to improve opportunity, increase inclusion, and make education more accessible.

ALPHABET

In 2015, Page, Brin, and then chairman Schmidt restructured Google. It became just one part of a new umbrella corporation called Alphabet. Its purpose was to allow Google to function without all its separate pieces getting in each other's way. Other parts of Alphabet include Calico, a biotech research company, and Waymo, a company that develops autonomous cars.

Page explained, "Alphabet is mostly a collection of companies."[13] Google is the largest of those companies. Sundar Pichai, a Google manager and executive since 2004, became Google's new CEO following the restructuring. The creation of Alphabet means that he

Sundar Pichai frequently appears onstage at new product unveilings and other important company events.

can focus all his efforts on Google instead of on the company's various side projects. In effect, the transition was intended to let Google be Google.

CHAPTER EIGHT

INTO THE FUTURE

Reaching for the impossible has always been a goal of Google's founders. Page famously said in 2013, "If you're not doing some things that are crazy, then you're doing the wrong things."[1] For this reason, the company often takes on a large number of forward-thinking projects, even if many of them are not likely to pan out.

Some of its developments, successful and unsuccessful, were due to the 20 percent time offered to employees. Eric Schmidt, CEO when 20 percent time was introduced, said that the policy was partly a tool for employees to push back against bad managers. If an employee felt too pushed, he or she could "legitimately look that boss in the eye and say, 'I'll give you 100 percent of my 80 percent time.'"[2]

Marissa Mayer, an ex-Googler and former Yahoo! CEO, has said, "I've got to tell you the

Google opened its new Asia headquarters in Singapore in 2016. Across the globe, the company's tens of thousands of employees are making advances on many fronts.

dirty little secret of Google's 20 percent time. It's really *120 percent* time."[3] Especially in Google's earlier years, there was a great deal of pressure for employees to work more than the standard 40 hours every week.

This 20 percent time was not really 20 percent of the total, but instead added to an employee's existing workload. In 2011, Page, having taken over as CEO from Schmidt, said that the company would be putting more energy into fewer, more specific, Google-related directions. And in 2013, Google placed some restrictions on who gets 20 percent time and for what. By then, employees and company outsiders argued that the practice was not even really used. Some employees said they had so much work to do, they didn't have time to take a day to work on something else.

GOOGLE FLU TRENDS

For all the 20-percent-time projects Google develops, some are bound to fail. Google Flu Trends is one that's often considered unsuccessful. The idea was to use Google search queries to track flu cases as they arose. It used that data to predict where outbreaks might soon occur. Flu Trends was fairly accurate in the beginning, but it became more skewed over time. Yet the experiment was not in vain. When Google's predictions were combined with Centers for Disease Control (CDC) predictions, the result was more accurate than either data set alone. In 2015, Google announced that it would give its data to health organizations to use for their own predictions. Since then, similar tests have predicted dengue fever outbreaks in Latin America.

Despite these changes, Google continues to innovate. Even established projects are proving useful in new and unexpected ways. For example, some individuals use Google Street View to boost tourism to little-known areas. Street View, part of Google Maps, allows users to see images of an area as though they were standing there. But Street View cameras can't travel everywhere. Most of the Faroe Islands, between Norway and Iceland, are an example. They have few roads. In 2016, Durita Dahl Andreassen attached solar-powered 360-degree cameras to the backs of a few of the islands' 80,000 sheep. When Google heard about the project, it loaned equipment to help. In late 2017, the Faroe Islands arrived on Google Street View.

In 2018, the city of Odate, Japan, added a dog's-eye view of the city to encourage tourism. Akitas wore cameras on harnesses and walked around the city, visiting local landmarks and attractions. Several museums around the world, including the National Museum of Scotland and the Palace of Versailles in France, use Street View technology. People around the world can explore them through Google's Arts & Culture platform.

Google has collaborated with museums to incorporate virtual reality into their exhibits.

HEALTH RESEARCH

With the company's restructuring, two health and research companies became independent under Alphabet. One of them, Calico, intended to focus its more than $1 billion in funding on studying aging and age-related illnesses. Much of what Calico does has not been made public. This frustrates researchers who would like to collaborate with Calico's researchers or focus on questions Calico isn't trying to answer. According to the company's chief science officer, "There will be nothing to say for a very long time, except for some incremental scientific things."[4] He estimates that Calico might have something big to announce around 2025.

The other health company, Verily, was formerly known as Google Life Sciences. It is now a separate company under Alphabet, working on biotechnology. It has been described as "kind of like Google for the human body."[5] One of Verily's largest projects is Project Baseline. After gathering the medical records of 10,000 healthy volunteers, Verily wants to analyze the data to get a baseline reading of what is average for the human body.

In 2014, Google applied for a patent for technology that would allow contact lenses to check blood sugar levels in people with diabetes. The company patented iris-scanning security contact lenses the following year. Also in the works at Verily is a machine that can determine an individual's risk of certain diseases by looking in their eyes. Verily's eye-scanning program requires much more work, but the project is promising.

To fight outbreaks of deadly mosquito-borne diseases such as Zika, dengue fever, and malaria, Verily has begun a project called Debug. Debug is meant to decrease the number of illness-carrying mosquitoes. In 2017, Verily bred and released millions of mosquitoes in the Fresno, California, area. Only males, which don't bite, were released. Each carried bacteria that naturally infect mosquito populations. The same bacteria make the males unable to reproduce. Any female mosquitoes that were to mate with these infected males would not produce eggs that could hatch. This would decrease the mosquito population over time. This might sound good for humans, but there are potential downsides. Scientists are studying how the program might affect species that eat mosquitoes.

GOOGLE X AND ITS SPIN-OFFS

Much of Alphabet's future profit potential may come from Google X. As the experimental arm of the company, it is Google X's job to come up with innovations. Google Glass, made available to the public in 2014, was among Google X's best-known creations. The device, worn like eyeglasses, can respond to voice commands and bring up videos and text before the wearer's eyes.

After about a year, Google stopped selling Glass to the general public. Part of the problem was concern for privacy and safety. Some people refused to even talk with someone wearing Google Glass, since the device has a built-in camera. But some workplaces found Google Glass useful for employees who need hands-free access to data, especially in manufacturing. Other companies developed their own versions of the Glass software to customize the devices for their employees, keeping Google Glass alive. The device may return to more widespread use someday. People are becoming more interested in augmented reality, a field of technology that involves overlaying digital information onto a person's view of the real world. Glass or something like it may become popular soon. And even if it doesn't, as Brin famously said in 2003, "The only way you are going to have success is to have lots of failures first."[6]

Google X has had successes, too. Beginning in 2009, Google X's self-driving cars have undergone extensive

FORMER GOOGLE X PROJECTS

Google X isn't short of big projects, but not all of them prove beneficial to the company. Cancelled X projects include Project Ara, a modular smartphone that can be swapped out piece by piece. It was abandoned in 2016. Boston Dynamics, a robotics company, was purchased by Google in 2013 and developed a robot that can move roughly like a human. It can even stand itself back up when it falls and carry and use objects. But Google ended up selling Boston Dynamics in 2016. Foghorn, a project making carbon-neutral fuel out of seawater, was too expensive to be useful. It was also dropped.

Google Glass was withdrawn from the public market after a few months, but it continued to be used in specialized industrial applications.

simulated and real-world testing. Like Google's search engine, the more use self-driving cars get, the more information they gather and the better they will perform. In 2016, Alphabet announced that Google's self-driving car project would be spun off into a new self-driving car company, Waymo. In 2018, Waymo announced its intention to start a driverless taxi service in Phoenix, Arizona. People had already been taking test rides in the cars there for more than a year.

Most Americans say they don't feel safe riding in a self-driving car. There will always be situations in which the car's computer doesn't know what to do. And the more companies such as Waymo test their self-driving cars, the more accidents will happen. Companies claim that when all or most cars drive themselves, the rate of collisions will be much lower. Computer-driven cars behave much more predictably than humans do. However the public might feel about them, self-driving cars are not going away anytime soon.

REMOTE-CONTROLLED CARS?

Some self-driving car companies are maintaining or developing remote driving capabilities, so a real person can take over from hundreds of miles away if needed. If one of Waymo's vehicles comes across something it doesn't recognize, the car will automatically request confirmation from a remote office location. Once it hears back from the office, the car's computer will decide what to do. This won't stop all collisions, but hopefully it will minimize damage. It should also help the car learn.

PROJECT LOON

One of Google X's biggest programs is Project Loon. The company announced plans in 2013 to provide internet access to the world using balloons flying about 12 miles (20 km) above the earth.[7] That's higher than any major storms that could knock out cell towers on the ground. According to project leader Mike Cassidy, each balloon can provide a signal to an area larger than Rhode Island.

But another company, Space Data, has been offering wireless services from its collection of balloons since 2004, well before Project Loon. Space Data has alleged that Google stole its ideas, and it sued Alphabet for patent infringement. The US Patent Office has even canceled one of Alphabet's patents because it was too similar to a patent Space Data already held. This will make Google's position harder to defend in the trial that's set for 2019.

While the technology may be similar to another company's, the intended use for that technology is unique to X. Project Loon's goal is to provide free wireless internet access for developing nations. Testing started in 2013 with balloons in New Zealand, Australia, and Latin America. Web access for everyone around the world is a vital component of making all knowledge accessible for everyone. But Google has something to gain from it, too. The more people who have access to the internet, the more people will likely use Google Search and the rest of the company's products.

Over one-half of the world's population is online. According to Tim Berners-Lee, the creator of the World Wide Web, "If we do not invest seriously in closing this

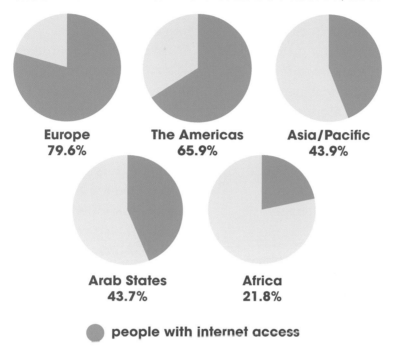

PERCENTAGE OF POPULATION ONLINE BY REGION, 2017[9]

Europe
79.6%

The Americas
65.9%

Asia/Pacific
43.9%

Arab States
43.7%

Africa
21.8%

people with internet access

gap [between those with internet access and those without], the last billion [people] will not be connected until 2042. That's an entire generation left behind."[8] If Google had its way, everyone would be connected. For a company interested in organizing and cataloging all the world's data, the more people who are online, the better.

TIMELINE

1996
Larry Page and Sergey Brin develop a new web-searching tool that uses websites' popularity as part of its ranking algorithm.

1997
In August, Google goes live on the Stanford University website.

1998
Page and Brin leave school to form a company; Google moves off campus to Susan Wojcicki's garage.

2000
Google begins providing search for Yahoo!; AdWords goes live, with advertisers bidding for keywords.

2001
Eric Schmidt becomes CEO of Google, Inc.

2002
Google Books launches.

2004
Google launches Gmail, a free email service; Google raises $1.67 billion dollars in its initial public offering, the most of any tech company until that time.

2005
Google enters the mobile market when it buys the Android operating system; it also announces Google.org and releases Google Maps.

2006
Google buys YouTube for $1.65 billion; the company also opens an office in China.

2007
Google buys DoubleClick, sparking an antitrust lawsuit; the company also launches Google Translate.

2009
Google launches a self-driving car test program, later called Waymo.

2010

Google publicly announces its servers have been hacked by someone working on behalf of China; it shares the information it finds with the US government and companies that were also hacked.

2012

Google lobbies Congress along with other companies to defeat the Stop Online Piracy Act.

2013

Google announces Project Loon and starts testing how to supply wireless internet service to the world using a network of balloons.

2015

Google restructures itself under new parent company Alphabet, separating various ventures.

2017

Executives of Google, Facebook, and other companies are called to testify to Congress about false and misleading advertisements placed by foreign entities during the 2016 presidential campaign; Google announces it relies entirely on renewable energy for all of its global operations; against vocal opposition, the FCC repeals its 2015 regulations ensuring net neutrality.

2018

Google controls just under half of the US digital advertising market.

ESSENTIAL **FACTS**

KEY PLAYERS
FOUNDERS
- Larry Page, Sergey Brin

CEOs
- Eric Schmidt (2001–2011)
- Larry Page (2011–2015)
- Sundar Pichai (from 2015)

KEY STATISTICS
- Google has more than 72,000 employees and made more than $19 billion in profit in 2017.
- Users run 40,000 web searches on Google.com every second. That's more than three billion searches every day.
- As of 2017, Google handled 80 percent of the world's web searches.
- Google has offices in 25 cities in North America and other offices in more than 40 other cities around the world.
- Google's search page is offered in more than 120 languages.
- In 2017, Google's senior management was 46 percent female, a higher percentage than at any other Fortune 100 company.

IMPACT ON HISTORY

Google was founded in 1998. It quickly became the world's most popular search engine, and it has remained in that position ever since. The company has also made significant inroads in other areas, providing a vast number of people with services for email, mapping, video, news, and mobile operating systems. Many of these services are free, though the data that users create has significant value for Google. Google also became a dominant player in the online advertising industry by selling advertising space alongside its search results. The company invests in forward-looking research projects that could someday have a huge impact. Among these projects are initiatives to develop self-driving cars and an effort to provide internet access to the developing world.

QUOTE

"If you're not doing some things that are crazy, then you're doing the wrong things."

—*Larry Page*

GLOSSARY

algorithm
A set of steps followed to solve a mathematical problem or to complete a computer process.

angel investor
A wealthy person who invests a large amount of money in a new company.

antitrust
Designed to protect trade from monopolies or other unfair business practices.

CEO
Chief executive officer of a company; the person in a company with the most authority.

copyright infringement
The act of using copyright-protected materials without the permission of the creators of the original work or their representatives.

data center
A building designed to house large numbers of computers, with special attention paid to cooling systems, consistent electricity service, and network connectivity.

fiber-optic cables
Very thin strands of glass that use laser light to move a lot of data at high speed.

hack

To secretly get access to the files on a computer or network in order to get information or cause damage.

lobbying

Trying to convince government officials to vote in a certain way.

patent infringement

The act of using patent-protected inventions or processes without the permission of the creators or their representatives.

protocol

A system of rules that computer systems follow.

search engine

A site on the World Wide Web that uses software to locate keywords on other sites.

server

A computer in a network that is used to provide services to other computers in the network.

venture capital

Money invested or available to be invested in a new company or project.

ADDITIONAL **RESOURCES**

SELECTED BIBLIOGRAPHY

Arthur, Charles. *Digital Wars: Apple, Google, Microsoft, and the Battle for the Internet*. Kogan Page, 2012.

Battelle, John. *The Search: How Google and Its Rivals Rewrote the Rules of Business and Transformed Our Culture*. Penguin, 2005.

Levy, Steven. *In the Plex: How Google Thinks, Works, and Shapes Our Lives*. Simon & Schuster, 2011.

Vogelstein, Fred. *Dogfight: How Apple and Google Went to War and Started a Revolution*. Sarah Crichton Books, 2013.

FURTHER READINGS

Eboch, M. M. *Big Data and Privacy Rights*. Abdo, 2017.

Higgins, Melissa, and Michael Regan. *Net Neutrality*. Abdo, 2017.

Hulick, Kathryn. *Artificial Intelligence*. Abdo, 2016.

ONLINE RESOURCES

Booklinks
NONFICTION NETWORK
FREE! ONLINE NONFICTION RESOURCES

To learn more about Google, visit abdobooklinks.com. These links are routinely monitored and updated to provide the most current information available.

MORE INFORMATION

For more information on this subject, contact or visit the following organizations:

COMPUTER HISTORY MUSEUM

1401 N. Shoreline Blvd.

Mountain View, CA 94043

650-810-1010

computerhistory.org

The Computer History Museum features artifacts and information from throughout the computing age, including many objects from the era when Google was just getting started.

GOOGLE

1600 Amphitheatre Pkwy.

Mountain View, CA 94043

650-253-0000

google.com/intl/en/about/our-company

Google's website features more information about the company, its history, its current projects, and its values.

SOURCE **NOTES**

CHAPTER 1. ORGANIZING THE WORLD'S INFORMATION

1. "Alphabet." *Fortune*, 2018, fortune.com. Accessed 25 Feb. 2018.

2. "Google Search Statistics." *Internet Live Stats*, 2018, internetlivestats.com. Accessed 25 Feb. 2018.

3. "Search Engine Market Share." *Net Market Share*, 2018, netmarketshare.com. Accessed 25 Feb. 2018.

4. Matthew Eisner. "Google Search Traffic by Year through 2016." *Matthew Eisner*, 4 Mar. 2018, matteisn.com. Accessed 29 June 2018.

5. John Battelle. *The Search: How Google and Its Rivals Rewrote the Rules of Business and Transformed Our Culture*. Penguin, 2005. 72.

6. Charles Arthur. *Digital Wars: Apple, Google, Microsoft, and the Battle for the Internet*. Kogan Page, 2012. 39.

7. Arthur, *Digital Wars*, 12.

8. Richard L. Brandt. *Inside Larry and Sergey's Brain*. Penguin, 2009. 71.

CHAPTER 2. A NEW WAY TO SEARCH

1. Randall Stross. *Planet Google: One Company's Audacious Plan to Organize Everything We Know*. Free Press, 2008. 24.

2. Steven Levy. *In the Plex: How Google Thinks, Works, and Shapes Our Lives*. Simon & Schuster, 2011. 19–20.

3. John Battelle. *The Search: How Google and Its Rivals Rewrote the Rules of Business and Transformed Our Culture*. Penguin, 2005. 72.

4. Stross, *Planet Google*, 50.

5. Ken Auletta. *Googled: The End of the World as We Know It*. Penguin, 2009. 40.

6. Stross, *Planet Google*, 50.

7. Auletta, *Googled*, 45.

8. Battelle, *The Search*, 92.

9. Battelle, *The Search*, 127.

CHAPTER 3. HIRING AND GROWING

1. Richard L. Brandt. *Inside Larry and Sergey's Brain*. Penguin, 2009. 63.

2. Steven Levy. *In the Plex: How Google Thinks, Works, and Shapes Our Lives*. Simon & Schuster, 2011. 134.

3. Brandt, *Inside Larry and Sergey's Brain*, 56.

4. Charles Arthur. *Digital Wars: Apple, Google, Microsoft, and the Battle for the Internet*. Kogan Page, 2012. 12.

5. Levy, *In the Plex*, 143–144.

6. David A. Vise with Mark Malseed. *The Google Story*. Delacorte Press, 2005. 67.

7. "Data Center Locations." *Google*, 2018. google.com. Accessed 13 Mar. 2018.

CHAPTER 4. DRAMATIC EXPANSION

1. Richard L. Brandt. *Inside Larry and Sergey's Brain*. Penguin, 2009. 92.

2. Ken Auletta. *Googled: The End of the World as We Know It*. Penguin, 2009. 30.

3. Jonathan Taplin. *Move Fast and Break Things*. Little, Brown and Company, 2017. 6.

4. Hamza Shaban. "Google Parent Alphabet Reports Soaring Ad Revenue, Despite YouTube Backlash." *Washington Post*, 1 Feb. 2018. washingtonpost.com. Accessed 15 Mar. 2018.

5. "Google's Revenue Worldwide from 2002 to 2017." *Statista*, 2018. statista.com. Accessed 29 June 2018.

6. Charles Arthur. *Digital Wars: Apple, Google, Microsoft, and the Battle for the Internet*. Kogan Page, 2012. 59.

7. Taplin, *Move Fast and Break Things*, 6.

8. David A. Vise with Mark Malseed. *The Google Story*. Delacorte Press, 2005. 153.

9. Fred Vogelstein. *Dogfight: How Apple and Google Went to War and Started a Revolution*. Sarah Crichton, 2013. 95.

10. Vogelstein, *Dogfight*, 131.

11. Steven Levy. *In the Plex: How Google Thinks, Works, and Shapes Our Lives*. Simon & Schuster, 2011. 237.

12. Taplin, *Move Fast and Break Things*, 21.

13. Levy, *In the Plex*, 245.

14. Auletta, *Googled*, 152.

SOURCE **NOTES**
○ CONTINUED

CHAPTER 5. GOOGLE AROUND THE WORLD

1. "Kai Fu Lee." *Sina Weibo*, 2018. weibo.com. Accessed 29 June 2018.

2. Steven Levy. *In the Plex: How Google Thinks, Works, and Shapes Our Lives*. Simon & Schuster, 2011. 293.

3. Levy, *In the Plex*, 293.

4. Fei-Fei Li. "Opening the Google AI China Center." *Google*, 13 Dec. 2017. blog. google.com. Accessed 16 Mar. 2018.

CHAPTER 6. GOOGLE AND THE GOVERNMENT

1. Shane Harris. *@War: The Rise of the Military-Internet Complex*. Houghton Mifflin Harcourt, 2014. 172.

2. Kim Zetter. "Google Hack Attack Was Ultra Sophisticated, New Details Show." *Wired*, 14 Jan. 2010. wired.com. Accessed 29 June 2018.

3. Jonathan Taplin. *Move Fast and Break Things*. Little, Brown and Company, 2017. 127.

4. Fred Vogelstein. *Dogfight: How Apple and Google Went to War and Started a Revolution*. Sarah Crichton, 2013. 199.

5. Steven Levy. *In the Plex: How Google Thinks, Works, and Shapes Our Lives*. Simon & Schuster, 2011. 318.

6. Cecilia Kang. "In Protests of Net Neutrality Repeal, Teenage Voices Stood Out." *New York Times*, 20 Dec. 2017. nytimes.com. 17 Mar. 2018.

CHAPTER 7. INVESTING IN SOCIETY

1. Eric Schmidt and Jonathan Rosenberg, with Alan Eagle. *Google: How Google Workd*. Grand Central Publishing, 2014. 224.

2. Randall Stross. *Planet Google: One Company's Audacious Plan to Organize Everything We Know*. Free Press, 2008. 90.

3. Stross, *Planet Google*, 92–93.

4. Stross, *Planet Google*, 93–94.

5. Jonathan Taplin. *Move Fast and Break Things*. Little, Brown and Company, 2017. 260.

6. Joseph Ax. "Google Book-Scanning Project Legal, Says U.S. Appeals Court." *Reuters*, 16 Oct. 2015. reuters.com. Accessed 17 Mar. 2018.

7. Stross, *Planet Google*, 107.

8. Stross, *Planet Google*, 103.

9. "Countries in the World by Population (2018)." *Worldometers*, 22 Mar. 2018. worldometers.info. Accessed 22 Mar. 2018.

10. Richard L. Brandt. *Inside Larry and Sergey's Brain*. Penguin, 2009. 217.

11. "Accountability in Education: Meeting Our Commitments." *UNESCO*, 2017. unesco.org. Accessed 22 Mar. 2018.

12. "About Us." *Pratham Books*, n.d. prathambooks.org. Accessed 16 Mar. 2018.

13. Larry Page. "G Is for Google." *Alphabet*, n.d. abc.xyz. Accessed 15 Mar. 2018.

CHAPTER 8. INTO THE FUTURE

1. Steven Levy. "Google's Larry Page on Why Moonshots Matter." *Wired*, 17 Jan. 2013. wired.com. Accessed 23 Mar. 2018.

2. Andrea Huspeni. "Google's 20 Percent Rule Actually Helps Employees Fight Back against Unreasonable Managers." *Entrepreneur*, 7 June 2017. entrepreneur.com. Accessed 15 Mar. 2018.

3. Nicholas Carlson. "The 'Dirty Little Secret' About Google's 20% Time, According to Marissa Mayer." *Business Insider*, 13 Jan. 2015. businessinsider.com. Accessed 15 Mar. 2018.

4. Antonio Regolado. "Google's Long, Strange, Life-Span Trip." *MIT Technology Review*, 15 Dec. 2016. technologyreview.com. Accessed 22 Mar. 2018.

5. Nicole Kobie. "The Future According to Alphabet Moonshots: From Calico to X." *Alphr*, 12 Jan. 2018. alphr.com. Accessed 17 Mar. 2018.

6. David A. Vise with Mark Malseed. *The Google Story*. Delacorte Press, 2005.

7. "Project Loon." *Google X*, n.d. x.company. Accessed 25 Feb. 2018.

8. Alan Martin. "Tim Berners-Lee: Google and Facebook Are Helping to Weaponise the Web." *IT Pro*, 12 Mar. 2018. itpro.co.uk. Accessed 15 Mar. 2018.

9. "ICT Facts and Figures." *International Telecommunications Union*, 2017. itu.int. Accessed 29 June 2018.

INDEX

ABOUT THE **AUTHORS**

AUDREY DeANGELIS

Audrey DeAngelis has worked as a living-history interpreter and an archaeologist. She is studying for a PhD in anthropology. She cowrote this book using about a dozen Google products.

GINA DeANGELIS

Gina DeAngelis writes books, articles, and screenplays for young people (and older ones) on many subjects. She first wrote about tech in 1997, and she remembers one day reading a news article that suggested people try this new search engine that was way better than all the others.

ABOUT THE **CONSULTANT**

ANTHONY ROTOLO

Anthony Rotolo was a college professor for more than ten years, teaching at Syracuse University. He taught courses in technology and media, including the very first college class on social media. He is now studying for a PhD in psychology and researching how social media affects people and society.